# THESSALONIKE
## MUSEUM

Publishers: George A. Christopoulos, John C. Bastias
Translation: L. Turner
Editor: Iris Douskou
Art Director: Angela Simou
Special Photography: I. Iliadis, M. Skiadaressis, S. Tsavdaroglou

# THESSALONIKE
## MUSEUM

**MANOLIS ANDRONICOS**
Professor of Archaeology
at the University of Thessalonike

**EKDOTIKE ATHENON S.A.**
Athens 1996

ISBN 960-213-015-6

Copyright© 1981, 1982
by
*Ekdotike Athenon S.A.*
*1, Vissarionos St., Athens 106 72*
*Printed in Greece*


PRINTED AND BOUND IN GREECE
by
EKDOTIKE HELLADOS S.A.
An affiliated company
8, Philadelphias Street, Athens

# CONTENTS

# INTRODUCTION
# HISTORY AND ART IN MACEDONIA

The Museum of Thessalonike might be described as the National Archaeological Museum of Northern Greece; like its Athens counterpart, it was the first museum to be built after the liberation of the region from Turkish rule in 1912. For many years, before the other Northern Greek cities acquired suitable museums of their own, the Museum of Thessalonike was the place where all the archaeological finds of Macedonia and Thrace were collected and exhibited.

## Prehistoric times in Northern Greece

Northern Greece has a very long cultural history, beginning at the dawn of prehistory, while its more recent chapters were irradiated by "our glorious Byzantinism", to recall the words of the poet Cavafy. As mentioned in the introduction to this volume, the presence of the human species in Greece since remotest antiquity was confirmed by the discovery of a skull at Petralona, in the Chalkidike peninsula, 30 kms. from Thessalonike. Anthropologists identified this skull as belonging to Neanderthal man, who is believed to have lived on the European continent 75-50 thousand years ago. Moreover, man-made tools ascribed to the Palaeolithic age were found in Thrace. Northern Greece may thus be considered the cradle of human history as far as Greece is concerned. But in the second phase of prehistory as well, that which scientists have named the "great revolution" because of the expansion of Neolithic civilization which occurred at that time, Macedonia may

aspire to first place owing to the very early and important settlement of
Nea Nikomedeia, near the town of Veroia; this is believed to be the
most ancient Neolithic settlement in the whole of Greece. From that
age onwards, an ever increasing number of finds over the whole
expanse of Macedonia and Thrace has enabled us to follow all the
successive stages of Neolithic civilization without interruption. Prehistoric settlements have been brought to light in quick succession from
Servia in Western Macedonia to Paradimi in Thrace (near Komotini),
and from Armenochori near Florina to the shores of the Chalkidike
peninsula.

   We must remember that when the earliest Hellenic tribes reached
Greece, Macedonia was the first area they encountered; a section of
these tribes, known as the *"Makednon ethnos"* and sometimes identified
with the Dorians, remained in the north of Greece and took root there.
I believe it is not in the least unlikely that these tribes remained in the
north over a long period of time, before the main bulk proceeded
south. This hypothesis may explain the vital significance of the great
Macedonian mountain, Olympos - the seat of the gods - in Greek
religion. Next to Olympos, another mountain-range known as the Pieria mountains, were thought by the Greeks to be the abode of the
Muses, those mythical beings who were the personification of culture.


## From the Mycenaean age to the Archaic period

   Like the inhabitants of several other Greek regions - Akarnania, for
instance - the Macedonians lived for many years isolated from the great
centres of Hellenism, but without quite losing contact with them.
Although Mycenaean finds in Macedonia have so far been scanty, they
provide evidence of some contact with the rest of the Hellenic world, a
contact which was to grow in the centuries that followed. The Protogeometric style, which emerged in Athens in the 11th century B.C. and
rapidly spread to nearly all the regions of Greece, eventually reached
Macedonia as well, as we can ascertain from the existence of a local
workshop, which was very probably influenced by similar workshops
in Thessaly and the Cyclades. Examples of pottery of this period are
cropping up in increasing quantity as archaeological excavations in
Macedonia have intensified in recent years and shed more and more
light on the early phases of historic times. It is hoped that research
might be equally rewarding with respect to the Geometric age, which is
not very well represented at present in the museums of Northern
Greece. This is due to chance and to the fact that very few excavations

have been undertaken so far in the north, for, both at Karabournaki, in Thessalonike, and at Nea Anchialos, a few kilometres west of Thessalonike, where limited investigations have been conducted, a large number of sherds from Geometric vases were discovered, carrying on the Protogeometric tradition in an unbroken line. More abundant still were pieces of Corinthian pottery, which conquered the markets of the Hellenic world, both east and west, in the 7th and early 6th centuries B.C., thanks to the commercial activity of Corinth at that time, but was displaced from the 6th century B.C. onward, by the products of Attic workshops. Attic vases of every period have been found in Macedonia, and the Museum of Thessalonike contains many remarkable examples of this art, providing evidence of a direct and close contact between the Northern Greek region and the great centre of ancient Greece.

**The influence of Ionic art in Northern Greece**

In the Archaic period, the wealthy Ionian cities in Asia Minor and on the large islands of the eastern Aegean occupied a very special place in the history of Greek civilization. We all know that Ionia was the cradle of Greek philosophy; to this day, the Ionian philosophers exert a particular fascination on the modern mind, owing to their surprisingly daring theories and the power and depth of their thought. We cannot help noting, however, that the artistic production of Ionia is not as well-known as it deserves to be, and the same can be said of the influence of the Ionian workshops on the rest of Greece. It is enough to mention that in the very heart of the Dorian world, in Sparta itself, the famous monument known as the "Amyklaian throne" was made by the Ionian Bathykles. This influence was particularly strong in all the areas north of Attica; from Boiotia to Thrace, sculptural works of the Archaic and even the early Classical period bear the vivid stamp of the Ionian spirit. But apart from the plastic arts, the influence of Ionic art in general on Northern Greece is indubitable. On the island of Thasos, at Neapolis on the opposite coast (modern Kavala), at Therme (Thessalonike), Ionic buildings occupy first place among the architectural creations of the Archaic period. Furthermore, the presence of Greek art was not restricted to the coastal areas, nor did it vanish with the end of the Archaic world, as the visitor may ascertain when going through the various rooms of the Museum of Thessalonike. This is evidenced even more convincingly by the Archaic kouros discovered at Kilkis, another smaller kouros found in the region of Pieria, and above all, a fine marble metope of the Classical period discovered at Aedonochori,

9

near the town of Serrai and exhibited at present in the Museum of Kavala. The metope is a splendid remnant of a Doric temple which must have been on a par with the temples of Southern Greece, judging from the exquisite modelling of the relief figures that adorn it.

### The rise of the Macedonian Kingdom and the foundation of Thessalonike

The growth and prosperity achieved by Macedonia during the reigns of Philip and Alexander are well-known. In the introductory note to the Museum of Pella, there has been mention of the fact that even before those two illustrious kings, another less-known king, Archelaos (413-399 B.C.) embellished his new capital, Pella, not only with works of art, but with the presence of the most famous intellectuals of Greece, not least among them Euripides, who wrote four of his great tragedies in Macedonia and ended his life there. At this point we should perhaps stress the significance of the foundation of Thessalonike by Kassandros in 316 B.C. Whereas Pella did provide a possible opening to the sea, the new historical conditions of the Hellenistic period demanded the creation of a coastal city with a safe harbour, allowing immediate communication by sea with all the other great ports of the eastern Mediterranean. The subsequent history of Thessalonike fully justifies Kassandros' choice of site. During both the Hellenistic and Roman periods, Thessalonike played a primary role in the political and cultural history of Macedonia, attested by written sources and the monuments housed in the Museum. Later still, when the Roman empire shrank to its eastern part, where it gradually grew into the vast Byzantine state, Thessalonike was known as the *symbasileuousa* (the co-reigning city), almost equal in importance to Constantinople. It is the only city in the Byzantine empire that has preserved an uninterrupted series of typical examples of Byzantine architecture, from the 5th to the 14th century A.D., which makes it the most vital and exciting museum of Byzantine art.

The fascination of Byzantine monuments and their admirable mosaics, beginning with the Rotunda, which dates from the 4th century A.D., and ending with the church of the Holy Apostles, which offers us late examples of mosaic art dated to the 14th century A.D., leave the traveller little time or inclination to complete his sight-seeing with a visit to the Archaeological Museum. Yet such a visit would not only give a full picture of the city's artistic life, but would also allow him to follow the historical and cultural evolution of Hellenism throughout Northern Greece.

# THE EXHIBITS
# IN THE MUSEUM OF THESSALONIKE

**Prehistoric exhibits**

The first important group of exhibits consists of Prehistoric finds from Macedonia and Thrace. Displayed here until recently were the numerous Neolithic vases found at Paradimi, in Thrace (near Komotini), during the first excavation carried out by the Faculty of Philosophy of the University of Thessalonike, under the direction of Stratis Pelekidis and Stilpon Kyriakidis. Although these finds have not yet been subjected to systematic study, they can be ascribed with some confidence to the last phase of Neolithic age. The fact that such a considerable number of vases (about 200 in all), quite often of large size, have survived intact from such a remote period of antiquity, is in itself very significant. Their diversity and the functional conception of their shape speak of a civilization with remarkable development and of a society that was already well beyond the first stages of organization. This collection has since been transfered to the Museum of Komotini.

Of a special interest is a group of exhibits, consisting of the finds from the cemetery of Vergina, near Veroia, makes up a unique collection of the early Iron Age (1000 - 700 B.C.), as the period corresponding to the Geometric times has been termed. Approximately 500 vases, of over 50 different shapes, give a clear picture of the artistic skill of those ancient inhabitants of Macedonia, as well as their relations and contacts with other places; for instance, a large number of vases in the collection are Protogeometric in style, beautifully and simply decorated with concentric circles and semicircles; as is well-known, this style originated in Attica. Then there are two vases of Mycenaean shape, several ceramic pieces which are almost certainly related to the art of Central Europe, and finally a large vase decorated in three colours, indicating that it came from Cyprus. There are also several hundreds of bronze ornaments, found in women's tombs. Beautiful spectacle fibulae, multispiral bracelets, rings, hair-ornaments, a diadem, double axes and several *omphalia* from belt-clasps, are among the most typical examples. Finally, iron weapons, swords, knives, spear-heads etc., provide the other side of the picture and complete our knowledge of the people, the social structure and the civilization of the Macedonian community during the early centuries of the 1st millennium B.C.


## The finds at Olynthos

The collection of finds from Olynthos has multifold importance. This well-known city of the Chalkidike peninsula, which acquired fame through the great speeches of Demosthenes, was built in 432 B.C. and destroyed in 348 B.C. by Philip of Macedon. American excavations have uncovered a large section of the city revealing the best preserved Greek city of the Classical age. Built according to a well-defined plan, known as the "Hippodameian system", with broad rectilinear avenues intersected by narrower streets, with regular building blocks consisting of ten houses each, with an admirable water-supply and sewerage system with bath-tubs wash-basins and lavatories of a surprisingly modern form, Olynthos provides tangible proof of the high standard of living of the ancient Greeks, and permits a reconstruction of their private life on the basis of concrete data. Unfortunately, the most important finds at Olynthos, the floor mosaics that have survived in excellent condition, are not accessible to archaeologists or antiquarians. These are the oldest mosaics in the history of Greek art. Several years ago a layer of soil was thrown over them in order to protect them, and they now await the time when they will once again emerge into the light of day and offer themselves to man's admiring gaze. The other finds of Olynthos, however, household utensils, vases, jewellery, weapons, tools, domestic cult objects etc., are all exhibited in the Museum of Thessalonike (figs. 58-59, 23-24).


## Sculptures from the Archaic and Classical ages

This Museum, like most other Greek museums, shelters within its walls characteristic works of art that are an integral part of the history of Greek art, but at the same time throw an unexpected light on the local history of the region. As already mentioned, Thessalonike was founded by Kassandros in 316-315 B.C., on the site of ancient Therme. During the Archaic period, Therme was an important city, with a clearly Greek character and culture; this has been ascertained irrefutably by the splendid, impressive remains of a large Ionic temple that stood at the centre of the site presently occupied by the city of Thessalonike. Ionic capitals, marble door-frames, Ionic and Lesbian *cymatia* and a small relief fragment (fig. 53), dating from approximately 500 B.C., are all examples of a robust Ionic architecture, comparable to the best of this kind produced in Ionia itself, or the Cyclades and corresponding to those found at Kavala.

Two Archaic statues - a clothed kouros and a kore - brought along by the refugees from Eastern Thrace, belong to the same period and the same Ionian world. From Western Thrace we have a fine funerary stele of the mid-5th century B.C., which is the product of some Cycladic workshop. Even in areas much nearer Thessalonike, archaeologists have discovered works testifying to the living presence of Greek art - Ionic in particular - and its extensive influence as far south as Boiotia. One of the finest and most recent acquisitions of the Museum is a funerary stele from Nea Kallikrateia in the Chalkidike peninsula. It belongs to a series of outstanding Cycladic gravestones of the "severe style" and the early Classical period, representing young girls. The Thessalonike stele represents a young girl holding a dove, her head slightly inclined forward. The skill and sensitivity of the island artist have succeeded in making the marble undulate and pulsate with life.

Works of secondary quality are certainly at a disadvantage next to this masterpiece. However, two other gravestones, of which only fragments have survived, are good enough to complete the overall picture of Northern Greek sculpture as it took shape under the influence of Ionia. One of these (fig. 57) was found in the area of Dion, the sacred city of the Macedonians at the foot of Mount Olympos, and the other (fig. 54) at Kassandra in the Chalkidike peninsula. The first shows a young girl's head, and is contemporary with the stele from Nea Kallikrateia; the second depicts a youth's head and dates from the end of the 5th century B.C.

To this group we must also add three works originating from three different areas of Macedonia. There is a funerary stele of the early 4th century B.C. (*c.* 370 BC.) showing a young lyre-player (fig. 55), which comes from the Chalkidike peninsula and still retains traces of Ionic influence. A second gravestone of the mid-4th century B.C. from Vergina, is inscribed with an epigram - which makes it one of the oldest inscriptions of Macedonia - and denotes that Attic art had by then replaced Ionian art as an influence in Northern Greece. This is corroborated by the third stele, which comes from Pieria, but is much inferior in quality.

## The Treasures of Vergina

The royal tombs of Vergina are now well known (fig. 1). The finds made during the excavations of 1977-78 are displayed in a special wing in Thessalonike Museum, and reveal the very high cultural level of the Macedonian kingdom in the years of Philip and Alexander. Even an inventory of the objects requires more space than the pages of this brief guide and it must be sufficient guidance for the visitor to indicate the main groups and to describe the most typical items in each.

The first group consists of the five grave *stelai* which, together with many others, were found broken into many pieces in the filling of the huge mound which covered the tombs. That bearing the relief figure of a warrior is one of the two sculptured *stelai of* the 5th century B.C. found in the kingdom of the Macedonians. The four others, with painted decoration, which are dated later than the middle of the 4th century B.C., provide very valuable historical information. The names of the dead, all of which are typically Greek, are decisive proof of the evidence already known from other historical sources, namely, that the Macedonians were one of many Greek tribes. They required no external influence to become hellenized, as some recent historians have tried to claim.

The other objects come from the two "macedonian" tombs, so far the only ones found unviolated. Most, and indeed the richest, items were found in the bigger of the two tombs, the one which the excavator believes to be that of Philip II, father of Alexander the Great. The finds are: 1) large and smaller bronze vesels; 2) silver vases; 3) two gold *larnakes,* gold jewellery and other gold articles; 4) the weapons of the deceased and 5) ivory figures from the decoration of wooden beds which in twenty-three centuries had decomposed from the damp in the tomb. Finally, there is the unique gold and purple material which covered the cremated bones of the dead princess.

On grounds of quality it is difficult to select two or three objects to take preference over the others. Each is a veritable work of art, many are unique: for example, the bronze lantern (fig. 18) pierced by countless openings with silver decoration on the neck, the bronze *oinochoe* with the head of Medusa below the handle and the silver vases which are superior in material rather than in craftsmanship. Over and above the unrivalled elegance of the shapes, the sensitivity of the decoration and the delicate gilding of various parts, these vases give us the opportunity to admire the most perfect example of Greek sculpture of the 4th century B.C. in the heads of Silenus (fig. 19), Heracles and Pan which decorate the lower end of the handles.

As for the gold objects, our attention might well be caught by the precious material alone which, in the case of the two *larnakes* (fig. 3) and the large wreath (fig. 6), quite literally outweighs that of every other example known from Greek lands. Nevertheless, though this richness is sufficient to dazzle someone unfamiliar with Greek culture, it is not the most striking element. The special value of both *larnakes* and neck-piece is derived from the workmanship and decoration. The relief ornamentation of the *gorytos* (combined bow-case and quiver) with the dramatic scenes of warriors pursuing frightened women with children in their arms into the shrine under the gaze of the sacred statues conveys its own compelling narrative (figs. 7-8). This is a puzzling piece because until now such objects have been found only in Southern Russia, in tombs of Scythian princes renowned as archers. Thus unexpectedly, excitingly even, both doubt is sown and surprise born in the informed visitor. Artistic expression soars to new heights, and makes one forget entirely the glitter of the metal in the dazzling achievements of human sensitivity and skill demonstrated in the two gold wreaths, especially the woman's. In the latter, artistic feeling complements the thorough exploitation of natural beauty presented in innumerable flowers and leaves on symmetrically placed stalks to which the bees hovering above add a life-like touch. It is neither an empty figure of speech nor fulsome exaggeration to say that this wreath is the most beautiful ornament known to us from ancient Greece.

If any other single exhibit deserves to compel like attention, it is the fabric which survived in two pieces. The technical skill rivals the delicate conception of the decoration, and the masterly arrangement of patterns the sumptuousness of the material. It is superfluous to add that this ranks as yet another unique possession of the Museum of Thessalonike.

Only a few of the many ivory carvings which decorated the wooden beds found in the tomb have been put on display. They include two portraits of inestimable value: the bust of Alexander as a young man and another of his father Philip as a mature man. In addition to their significance as the only genuine portraits of the two rulers, they, together with the other rare examples of Greek portraiture of about the mid-4th century B.C., show the very high level attained by that branch of Greek sculpture which until now we knew only through Roman copies (figs. 13-17).

This resplendent picture of royal wealth and the high cultural standards of the Macedonian court during Philip's reign is amplified in the most unexpected way by the weapons of the dead man. All, from the most common - spear-heads - to the rarest - the cuirass (fig. !1) and the helmet (fig. 12) - are products of advanced technology and exceptional craftsmanship. Rust has deprived us of their former shine which may be imagined by looking at part of a spear-head whose surface has the hard glint of steel. Certainly the gold inlaid sword (fig. 10) with its ivory scabbard and the wholly original gold ornamentation of the cuirass make us forget the deterioration of the rest of the surface.

Surpassing all else in refinement, beauty and craftsmanship is the superb chryselephantine shield. Even though the decay of the frame (made of wood and leather) contributed to its disintegration and to the crushing of the ornamentation, which consisted of ivory, gold and glass, the accurate restoration of both the frame and a large part of the original surface allows us to appreciate this superlative object.

From the smaller tomb comes the unique collection of 29 silver vases, unmatched in any museum in the world. The artistic standard is high, although not equal to that of the vases found in the 'tomb of Philip'. Nonetheless, one at least is a master-piece. It has the shape of a deep frying-pan (called a *patera* by the Romans) and its long handle ends in the moulded head of a ram. The visitor who pauses to examine that head carefully cannot fail to observe that it is a small gem of Greek sculpture where the plastic treatment of the volume combined with deft, sure engraving and the help of gilding succeeds in rendering the shape of the animal with rare precision.

From the same tomb comes a pair of gilded greaves (fig. 9) and many gilded strigils, rare examples of their type, which testify to the fact that the dead youth was undoubtedly a member of the royal family. When the work of conservation on the wooden bed is complete, the visitor will be able to enjoy the finest piece of ivory sculpture to have survived from the ancient world; a small figure of Pan playing the flute followed by a dancing Dionysiac couple endowed with all the charm of Bacchic exaltation.

The written word is of slight assistance to the visitor as he stands in front of the objects themselves. His eyes and senses alone permit him to appreciate the priceless worth of the finds from Vergina. And though it must be regarded as superfluous, the writer of these lines would like to offer a word of advice: that the visit should not be made in haste and, if at all possible, should be repeated after an interval.


**The Krater of Derveni**

At Derveni, 10 kms. outside Thessalonike, tombs dating from the 4th century B.C. were discovered some twenty years ago by chance in the course of opening up the national highway linking Thessalonike to Kavala. These finds were both unexpected and unique, precursors of those made later at Vergina. The most important find has now become famous throughout the world, because it immediately took up an outstanding place in every history book of Greek art. The object in question, which has no equal in the world, is a large bronze krater, 0.91 m. high, covered with sculptured ornaments (figs. 32-35). There is an engraved inscription along its rim which reads: "ΑΣΤΕΙΟΥΝΙΟΣ ΑΝΑΞΑΓΟΡΑΙΟΙ ΕΣ ΛΑΡΙΣΑΣ". We are thus informed that the owner's name was Asteiounios, son of Anaxagoras, from Larisa. On the body of the krater we see a group of Silenoi and Maenads gathering in Bacchic ecstasy around the sacred couple, Dionysos and Ariadne. On its shoulders, there are four sculptured figures belonging to the Dionysiac *thiasos* (company): Dionysos himself with a Maenad (fig. 32) on one side, and a Silenos with a Maenad on the other. Within the volutes there are four bearded figures (fig. 34); the neck of the krater is decorated with twelve applied animals (deer, griffins, panthers, lions, etc.). The krater's reliefs betray supreme artistry, retaining all the nobility and refinement of Praxitelian creations, with the addition of a passionate, almost ecstatic quality which the craftsmen of the 4th century B.C. acquired from the great Parian sculptor Skopas.

Apart from the krater of Derveni, the visitor can admire several other bronze vases (figs. 40-45) and weapons (figs. 37-38), gold ornaments (figs. 2, 25-26, 30-31) and elegant glass vases (*alabastra*). But the most distinctive exhibits are undoubtedly a number of silver vases, both elegantly and audaciously shaped; the decoration is discreet and the workmanship of excellent quality (fig. 46). Finally, the tombs of Derveni have also yielded fragments of a papyrus scroll, the first, though neither the oldest nor the only one found on Greek soil. It is not the oldest surviving papyrus in Greek, but it cannot be very far apart, chronologically speaking, from the famous Timotheos papyrus, which is dated to the late 4th century B.C. The text of the papyrus consists of 18 verses from an Orphic poem with allegorical comments.

Before we proceed to the sculptures, it is worth taking note of the finds from another tomb, dug up in the town quarter of Neapolis. These finds consist of fine gold jewellery (bracelets, a necklace, earrings, etc.), terracotta statuettes, a glass vase and a faience vase. Like the krater of Derveni, this last item, of a beautiful green colour, with low-relief representations of Artemis and various animals, is unique in

*1. Aerial photograph of the Great Tumulus of Vergina* ▶

Greece (fig. 50). It is a product of Egypt at the time of the Ptolemies and one of the most admirable examples of this type of vase. It has been ascribed to the mid-2nd century B.C., this date being confirmed by the terracotta statuettes that were found with it.

### Roman copies of Classical works

Apart from these original creations, the Museum includes some Roman copies of well-known Greek Classical works. There is a colossal head of Athena; this head and the right foot are the only remains from the copy of a famous statue of Athena by Pheidias. Two other heads, whose high polish indicate they were made in Roman times, are most probably copies of works by the same great artist. The most important copy is a headless statue of Aphrodite, known under the Roman name of *Genetrix*. It is not only its fine craftmanship that places it in an outstanding position among the fifty other copies of this work scattered in various museums across the world; the Thessalonike example is of particular interest because it is the only one to have survived with its pedestal, thus enabling us to see it in its correct position. This simple fact is of fundamental relevance for a proper artistic appreciation of this work (fig. 60). On the basis of these details, we have good reason to suggest that the opinion shared by most archaeologists, attributing this work to Kallimachos, the famous sculptor of the 5th century B.C., must be revised.

### Roman sculpture

One of the most important contributions of the Museum of Thessalonike is the opportunity it offers both scholar and layman to admire one of the richest collections of Roman sculpture, dating from the 1st century B.C. to the end of antiquity. The numerous funerary and votive reliefs may not always be works of high quality, but the series of portraits can certainly claim first place in the art of portraiture, which thrived during that period. Among these portraits we must single out a 1st century B.C. head, which marks the transition from the artistic climate of the late Hellenistic period to the age of the Roman republic (fig. 64). The statue of Augustus (fig. 62), one of the innumerable statues of this kind set up in the various territories conquered by the Romans, is remarkable for its sturdy structure, its sensuous modelling and the well-balanced combination of the intellectual and military aspects in a single human personality. There is another outstanding portrait made of bronze and quite rare of its kind, representing Alexander Severus (A.D. 222-235), the boy who became emperor at 14, who enjoyed reading Plato's *Republic* and was responsive to the new religious currents from the East (fig. 65). Next to this boyish figure stands the portrait of a man in his maturity (fig. 63), which strikes us as rather coarse, weighed down by experience; he apparently lived during the terrible years that succeeded the dynasty of the Severi, the years of the Gordiani (A.D. 235-244). However, the most significant works, as regards the history of ancient sculpture, are three portraits belonging to the end of the ancient world. First, the statue of a venerable lady (fig. 68), who lived during the reign of Constantine the Great: this is one of the rare examples of sculpture of that late date. The spiritualized face, the introverted expression, the dreamy gaze reveal how radically, how irreversibly man's views had changed. The woman's body, enfolded in heavy draperies, has practically ceased to exist; it has become a shapeless stump, rather like a pillar, whose sole function is to support the head, which is where all the subject's expressiveness is now concentrated. There are two other busts portraying a man and a woman (figs. 66, 69); both these works carry to extremes the tendencies noted in the previous portrait. Dating to the turn of the 4th century A.D., they are the last examples not only of the art of ancient portraiture, but of ancient sculpture in general. We cannot help admiring the artist's ability in eliminating completely the material, physical aspect of his subject and transforming it into a vehicle for elusive states of mind. This is particularly true of the male figure, with its uncertain, enigmatic gaze, the imperceptible contraction of the lips, the modelling of the cheekbones, the intricate arrangement of the hair, and above all the unworldly expression of the face, which make it one of the most powerful portraits of any period.

The collection of sarcophagi is of considerable importance. Apart from the various examples decorated very simply with garlands, cupids, relief portraits of the dead, or representations of a religious character (for instance, there is a particularly interesting sarcophagus decorated with themes related to the cult of Isis), there are sarcophagi of the 2nd and 3rd centuries A.D., known as "Attic", elaborately decorated with mythological themes (fig. 67). These representations in relief are a continuation of the ancient tradition of Greek sculpture and indicate how familiar and popular was the world of myth even during the last centuries of antiquity. Orpheus among the wild beasts, the hunting of the Calydonian boar, Amazonomachies, Centauromachies, sea-battles and Dionysiac scenes *(thiasoi)*, (figs. 73-74) are the main subjects that inspired the artists who made these sarcophagi. There are instances when one can pick out among the reliefs certain figures which originate from famous Classical prototypes, proving how deep and permanent was that great flowering of the Greek spirit.

Among hundreds of secondary works, mostly small funerary or votive reliefs of the Roman age, which offer abundant and rewarding material to the student of the religion of those times, one can single out some exhibits which are unquestionably the work of plain craftsmen, yet display unusual sensitivity, sound technical knowledge and a certain artistic power, (figs. 70-72). First and foremost, we must mention a small relief portrait of a woman - part of a gravestone, no doubt - which immediately impresses the spectator with the simplicity of its features, the solidity of its modelling and the vigour of its expression. A second relief consists of the busts of a family group; the plastic modelling of the faces is quite remarkable: sharp edges, smooth simple planes, clear-cut geometric volumes, conveying a purely cubistic and modern impression. Finally, among the numerous relief sculptures picturing what has become known in the history of art and religion as a "Thracian horseman", there is a small figure, which for all its unsophisticated craftsmanship, shows how an age-old tradition in sculpture has been able to endow this ordinary, unimportant little object with nobility, confidence and ease. It may be worth while to make a systematic study of all such simple, unpretentious products of an art which one might describe as "popular", and to delineate the geographical boundaries within which the creations of these humble craftsmen maintained the old tradition of Greek sculptural skill, as opposed to some other areas of the Roman empire where the very same themes were rendered with all the coarseness and clumsiness resulting from the lack of such a historical heritage. A study of this kind would undoubtedly pinpoint those areas where Hellenism grew out of a deep and ancient tradition and was not the result of Hellenistic expansion or, to a much lesser degree, of Roman conquest. Anticipating such a study, we can already affirm that these areas extended in all directions, far beyond the frontiers of Greece as we know them today.


**Glass vases**

There is yet another collection in the Museum of Thessalonike which is sure to attract the attention of both scholar and layman: Roman glassware (figs. 51-52). Not all these exhibits are of a high quality, but they are typical and representative examples of ancient glasswork which set the foundations of the technique and eventually replaced both ceramic and faience products. Although nowadays our daily contact with glass objects has made us so familiar with this material that our aesthetic instinct does not always react as powerfully as it should at the sight of them, there are some ancient glass vases that immediately rouse our interest and exert a peculiar attraction. Those ancient glass-workers, full of the enthusiasm and vigour that came from discovering a new material, succeeded in giving their works daring new forms, alive and sensual. Terracotta prototypes did not hinder their inspiration; they supplied craftsmen with a starting-point, beyond which they could move forward, using their imagination and their responsiveness to the new material.

## Mosaics

The last exhibits awaiting the visitor to the Museum are the Roman floor mosaics discovered in Thessalonike. The largest and most important is a multi-figured composition from Dionysiac mythology; in the centre, we see Ariadne, reclining, and Dionysos approaching her; he is surrounded by various figures of the Dionysiac *thiasos* (company). Each separate figure, as well as the composition as a whole, displays the mosaicist's remarkable skill, technique and experience; in those days, his craft was highly developed throughout the Roman empire, as evidenced by the innumerable mosaics discovered all over the then known world, from the British shores to the regions of the East. Such mosaics can be found everywhere in Greece, from Nikopolis in Epeiros to the Aegean islands. The most recent finds are the famous mosaics of Mytilene, illustrating the comedies of Menander and including the poet's portrait. In the Museum of Thessalonike there is also a series of mosaics representing busts of male and female figures related to the mythology of the sea, as shown by the various symbols in the compositions: anchors, claws from crustaceans, etc. (figs. 75-76). However, as we have already remarked at the beginning of this text, anybody interested in mosaics need only visit the numerous architectural monuments of Thessalonike in order to follow the subsequent development of this art from the 4th century A.D., beginning with the Rotunda, going on to the churches of Hosios David, Saint Demetrios, the Acheiropoietos, Saint Sophia, and ending up with the Holy Apostles, where the mosaics of the Palaiologan renaissance bring us back to the Hellenistic sources, which nurtured Greek Christian art over the course of many centuries.

*2. Golden myrtle wreath from Derveni. Second half of the 4th century B.C.*

*3. The gold larnaca found in the chamber of the Great Tomb of Vergina. The bones it contained are most probably those of Philip II. The sides of the larnaca are decorated with plant motifs and its lid bears the star, emblem of the Macedonian dynasty.*

*4. Eight-pointed stars ornament the three gold discs found in the Great Tomb of Vergina.*

*5. The gilded silver diadem - probably worn by a king - from the Great Tomb of Vergina.*

-5

7

◄6. *The gold oak wreath found in the chamber of the Great Tomb. It is the most impressive ancient wreath which has been found to date.*

7. *A gold plate depicting scenes of battle in relief formed the decoration of the gorytos (a kind of bow-case and quiver). From the Great Tomb of Vergina.*

8. Detail of the above; the upper band shows a warrior and a woman with a child, the lower a woman who has reached the shelter of the sanctuary.

9. Gilded bronze greaves, from the Great Tomb of Vergina.

10. Hilt of the iron sword with gold decoration, from the Great Tomb of Vergina.

*11. Macedonian iron helmet, from the Great Tomb of Vergina.*

*12. The cuirass of the dead man, from the Great Tomb of Vergina. It is made of iron, relieved by gold bands of ornamentation.*

13-17. *The miniature ivory heads found in the chamber of the Great Tomb of Vergina. No. 13 depicts a mature bearded man, most probably Philip; no. 16 is Alexander and no. 15 perhaps represents Olympias.*

13

1

1

18. *The lantern, a bronze vessel pierced with holes. At the bottom an iron support held a clay lamp. From the Great Tomb of Vergina.*

19. *The head of Silenus on a silver vase. From the Great Tomb of Vergina.*

19

20. Cheek-piece of a bronze helmet with a relief representation of a winged Nike holding a spear and shield. 4th century B.C.

21. Detail from a silver hydria, a siren surrounded by plant decoration. From Torone, Chalkidike. End of the 5th century B.C.

23

24

22. *The head of a gorgon on the handle of a krater-situla. From Stavroupolis, Thessalonike. Second half of the 4th century B.C.*

23-24. *Details from a hammered bronze plaque from Olynthos. Above is a reclining nude young man, below a barbarian chieftain holding a sceptre. First half of the 4th century B.C.*

25-26. *Gold necklaces from Derveni. 4th century B.C.*

27. *A gold necklace from Sedes. 4th century B.C.*

28. *Gold oak wreath from the region of Amphipolis. 4th century B.C.*

29. *Detail from a gold thigh ornament with the magic knot of Heracles. From Sedes, Thessalonike. 4th century B.C.*

30. *Gold diadem with plant ornamentation. From Derveni. 4th century B.C.*

31. *Gold myrtle wreath from Derveni. Second half of the 4th century B.C.*

*32-33. The large bronze krater from Derveni with relief representations is
a work of exceptional beauty dating to 330 B.C. The volutes are decorated
with relief figures, such as Heracles, shown here (32).*

*32*

*34-35. Details from the Derveni krater, showing a seated maenad and a satyr with a dancing maenad.*

36. *Bronze helmet from Leukadia, Naoussa. 5th century B.C.*

37. *Leather neck-piece of a cuirass with attached bronze scales. From Derveni. 4th century B.C.*

38. *Greaves from Derveni. 4th century B.C.*

39. *The head and butt of a sarissa. The sarissa - a long spear - was the most typical weapon of the Macedonian phalanx.*

38

39

40

40. *Bronze amphora complete with lid. From Derveni. End of the 4th century B.C.*

41. *Bronze oinochoe from Derveni. End of the 4th century B.C.*

42. *Bronze situla from Derveni. End of the 4th century B.C.*

43. *Bronze kalyx from Derveni. End of the 4th century B.C.*

41

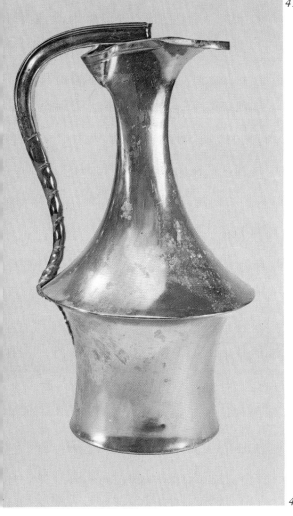

42

43

44

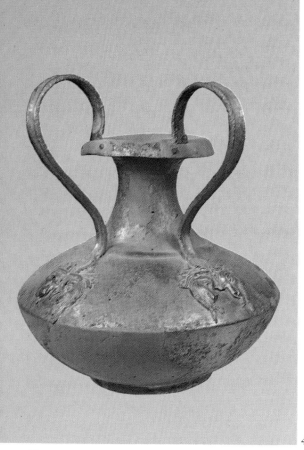

45

46

*44. Bronze amphora from Derveni. End of the 4th century B.C.*

*45. Bronze oinochoe from Derveni. End of the 4th century B.C.*

*46. Silver ethmos (strainer) from Derveni. The artist has exploited to the utmost the opportunity the precious metal afforded him to create elaborate forms. End of the 4th century B.C.*

*47. Lantern with moveable handles. The body is pierced to shed the light of the clay lamp which stood inside. From Derveni. Second half of the 4th century B.C.*

*47*

48. Gold medallion
with a portrait of
Olympias on one side
and a mounted
Nereid on the other.
It was probably
struck about the
middle of the 3rd
century A.D. when
the Olympic games
were held in
Macedonia.

49. Gold head of
Heracles, part of
some piece of
jewelry. From
Derveni. End of the
4th century B.C.

50. *A remarkable faience vase, unique in Greece. Its low relief surface shows many scenes, amongst them Artemis standing in a forest. It comes from Ptolemaic Egypt and was discovered in a grave of the 2nd century B.C. in Thessalonike.*

51-52. *Glass vases of the Roman period. This new material, with its range of delicate colours, gave craftsmen the chance to devise wonderful shapes.*

50

54

53. Archaic relief head, part of the sculpture decoration of a splendid Archaic temple which stood at the centre of the site of modern Thessalonike. Several architectural members, Ionic in style, from the same temple have also been found. c. 500 B.C.

54. Relief figure of a youth from a grave stele found at Kassandra, Chalkidike. Ionic influences were beginning to give way to the Attic style. End of the 5th century B.C.

55. Funerary stele of a young lyre-player, found in the area of Poteidaia in the Chalkidike peninsula. The modelling retains traces of the Ionic influence. c. 370 B.C.

56. *Grave stele from N. Kallikrateia, Chalkidike, a perfect example of the Cycladic style. It depicts a young girl with a dove. Early 5th century B.C.*

57. *Relief figure of a young girl from a grave stele found at Dion, Pieria. The Ionic influence is clear. About the middle of the 5th century B.C. Museum of Dion.*

57

*58-59. Clay mould of a protome bust of Cybele holding a cymbal. To the right the cast. From Olynthos. Beginning of the 4th century B.C.*

60

61

60. Headless copy of a statue of Aphrodite.

61. Head of a woman, dated to the reign of Hadrian.

62. Portrait statue of Augustus (27 B.C. - A.D. 14). The features of the great Roman ruler keeps the nobility and spirituality of earlier Greek portraits.

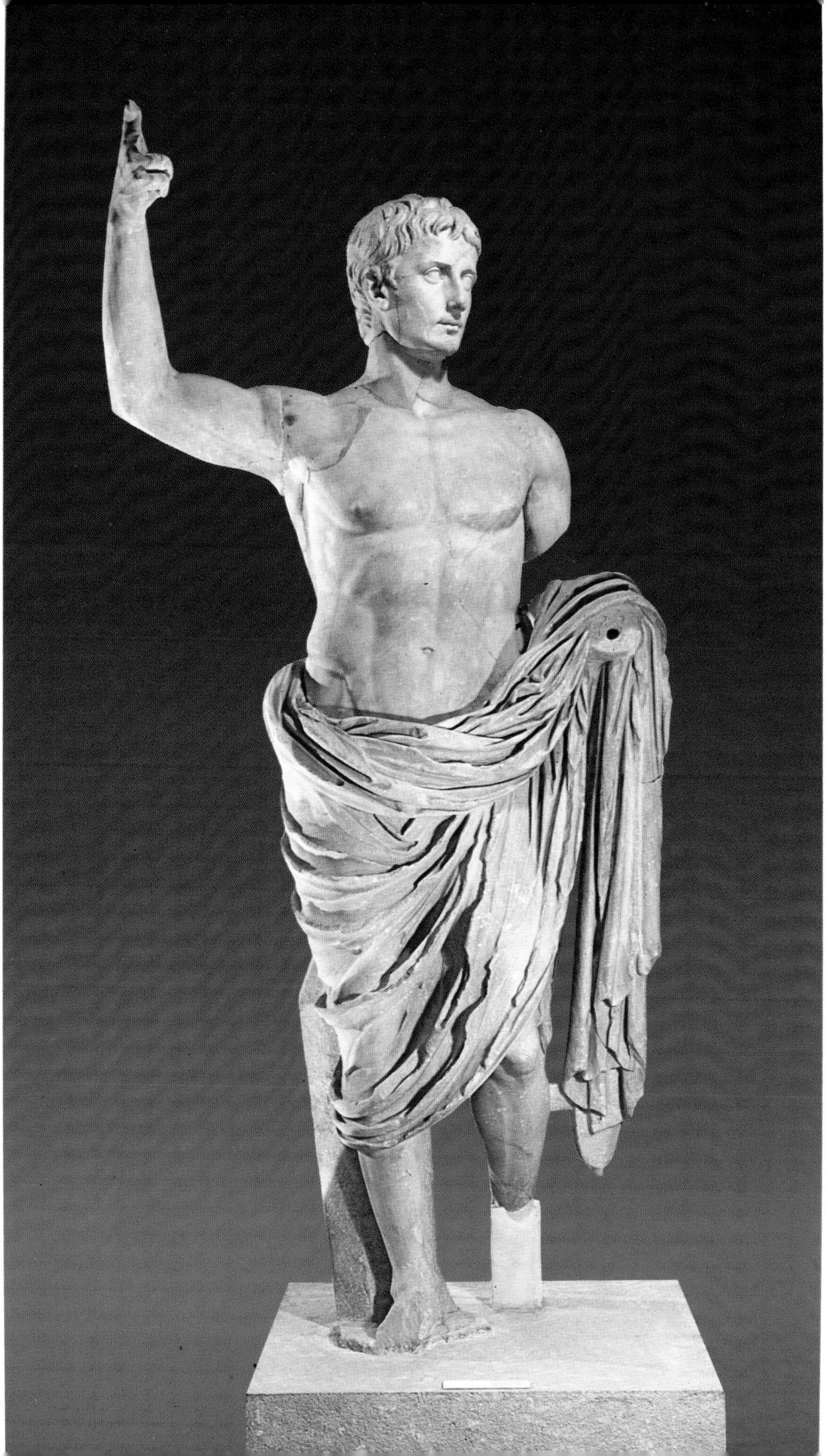

*63. Male portrait of the 1st century B.C. The vitality of the Hellenistic tradition has been successfully transmitted to works of the Roman republic.*

*64. Male portrait of the mid 3rd century A.D. The realism of the features is impressive and reflects the unrest prevailing in the Roman Empire.*

*65. Bronze portrait head of the Emperor Alexander Severus (A.D. 222 - 235), a superb example of imperial portraiture.*

65

66

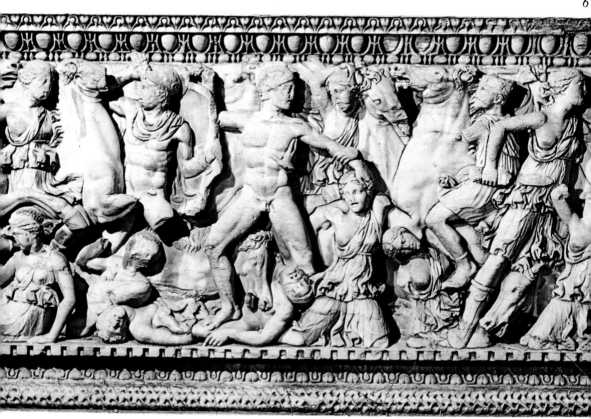

6

66. *Bust of a man, dating to the last years of the 4th century A.D.*

67. *Sarcophagus of the Roman imperial period with a representation of the Amazonomachy.*

68. *A statue portraying a Roman lady of the reign of Constantine the Great. This rare example of sculpture of late antiquity illustrates the radical transformation which took place in the plastic treatment of the human body.*

69. *Bust of a woman dated to the last years of the 4th century A.D. It represents the last flicker of the ancient world and presages a new era.*

69

70

71

70-71. *Grave relief
from Lete, depicting
men, women and
servants. It bears an
inscription with the
name of the artist.
1st century A.D.*

72. *Grave monument.
It depicts two men
with horses. 1st
century B.C.*

74

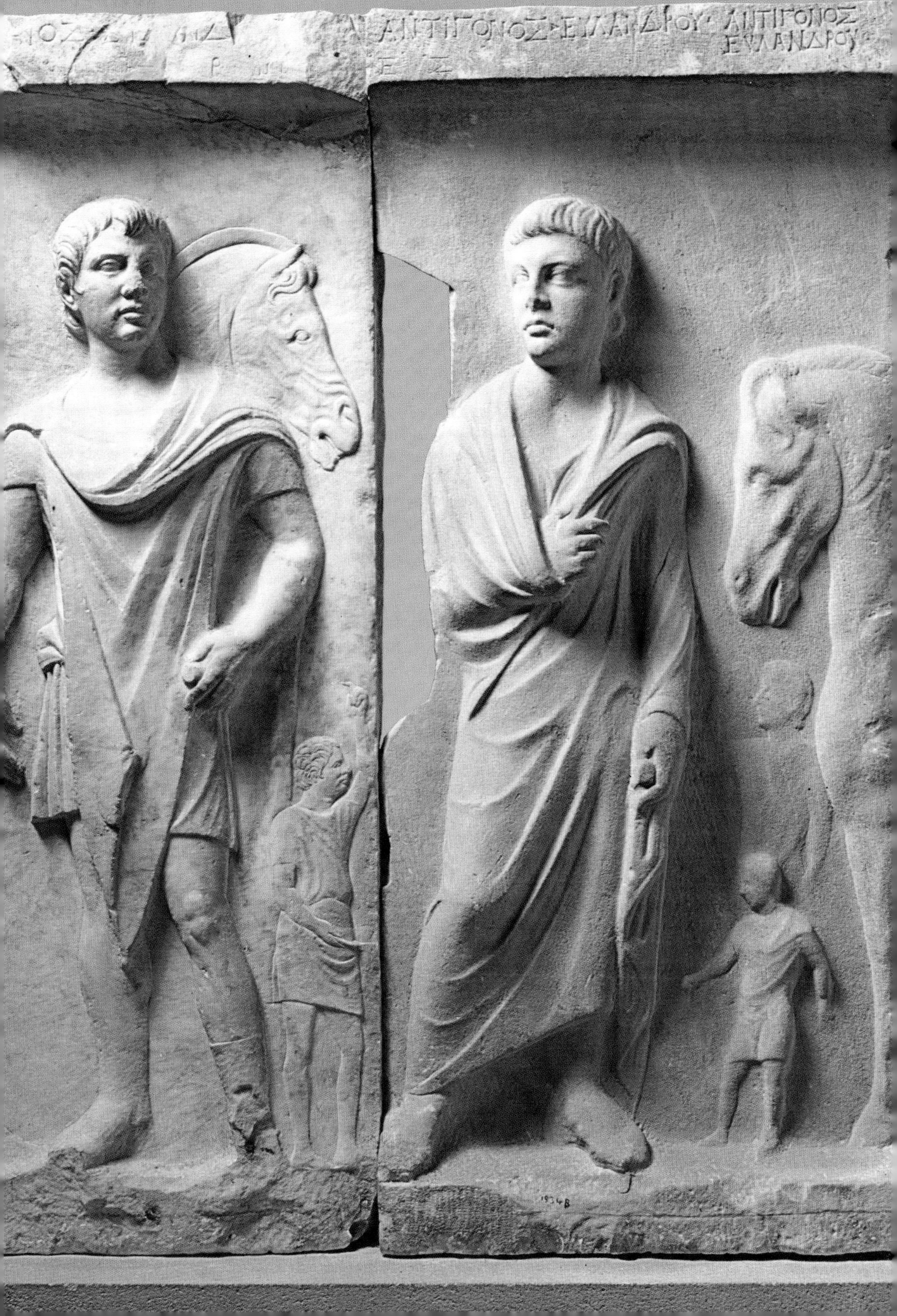
ΑΝΤΙΓΟΝΟΣ
ΕΥΑΝΔΡΟΥ

*73-74. Attic sarcophagus from the western cemetery of Thessalonike depicting Dionysiac themes, satyrs, maenads, figures of Eros and small children treading grapes.*

## 7

75. *Section of a mosaic floor of the Roman imperial period. A female figure symbolizes the marine world.*

76.*Fragment of a floor moaic of the Roman imperial period. A male figure sympolizes the marine world.*

ΥΠΟΥΡΓΕΙΟ ΠΟΛΙΤΙΣΜΟΥ

924705

ΤΑΜΕΙΟ ΑΡΧΑΙΟΛΟΓΙΚΩΝ ΠΟΡΩΝ

ΤΑΠ